CENGAGE Learning

# Novels for Students, Volume 26

**Project Editor**: Ira Mark Milne

**Editorial**: Jennifer Greve

**Rights Acquisition and Management**: Margaret Chamberlain-Gaston, Leitha Etheridge-Sims, Kelly Quin, Tracie Richardson **Manufacturing**: Drew Kalasky

**Imaging and Multimedia**: Lezlie Light **Product Design**: Pamela A. E. Galbreath, Jennifer Wahi **Vendor Administration**: Civie Green

**Product Manager**: Meggin Condino

*For more information, contact*
Gale
27500 Drake Rd.
Farmington Hills, MI 48331-3535

Or you can visit our Internet site at http://www.gale.com **ALL RIGHTS RESERVED**

*Permissions Department*
Gale
27500 Drake Rd.
Farmington Hills, MI 48331-3535
Permissions Hotline:
800-730-2214
Fax: 800-730-2215

of the editors or publisher. Errors brought to the attention of the publisher and verified to the satisfaction of the publisher will be corrected in future editions.

ISBN-13: 978-0-7876-8683-3
ISBN-10: 0-7876-8683-2
eISBN-13: 978-1-4144-2933-5
eISBN-10: 1-4144-2933-9
ISSN 1094-3552

Printed in the United States of America
10 9 8 7 6 5 4 3 2 1

# *The Tenant of Wildfell Hall*

## Anne Brontë

## 1848

## Introduction

*The Tenant of Wildfell Hall*, by Anne Brontë, is one of the first modern feminist novels. It tells the story of a young wife during the Regency period in England (1800-1830) who runs away from her drunken, adulterous, verbally abusive husband, an act virtually unheard of at this time in history. Brontë is the youngest sister of the famous Charlotte Brontë and Emily Brontë and although her poetry and novels have never received the same attention, she was arguably the pioneer of her family. Brontë's use of realism—unlike the gothic romances of Charlotte and Emily—was a precursor to the literary traditions of the late nineteenth and early twentieth centuries.

*The Tenant of Wildfell Hall* was a wildly popular and controversial novel when it was published in 1848. Critics then and later criticized the uneven characterization, but it was Brontë's progressive ideas about the rights of women that caused an uproar in the mid-1800s. Some considered the novel unfit for women to read. *The Tenant of Wildfell Hall* has interest for readers in the early 2000s because of its insight into the historical roles of men and women and for the ways it illustrates how marriage has changed and how some things—such as domestic abuse—have not.

Despite Faulkner's roots in the South, he readily condemns many aspects of its history and heritage in *Absalom, Absalom!*. He reveals the unsavory side of southern morals and ethics, including slavery. The novel explores the relationship between modern humanity and the past, examining how past events affect modern decisions and to what extent modern people are responsible for the past.

# Author Biography

Anne Brontë was born January 17, 1820, the sixth and last child of Patrick and Maria Branwell Brontë. She was born in the village of Thornton in West Yorkshire, England, but the family moved to Haworth just a few months later so that her father could take a higher paying position as the local parson. Brontë's mother died before her youngest daughter was two years old. Their aunt, Elizabeth Branwell, came to live with the family and cared for the children. She and Anne were particularly close as Aunt Branwell was effectively the only mother the girl remembered having. The two eldest daughters, Maria and Elizabeth, died when Anne was only four. Growing up, Anne was closest to her sister Emily, and together they made up stories about the imaginary land of Gondal. Charlotte and her brother Branwell similarly played together, making up stories about a fantasy land named Angria.

Anne Brontë did not attend school until she was fifteen when she took Emily's place at Roe Head School. She was acutely homesick but, unlike Emily, she endured being at school and worked hard because she believed an education would give her the means to support herself. Her first known poems were written during her two years at school. She worked as a governess for the Ingham family at Blake Hall in 1839 and then, in 1840, for the Robinson family of Thorp Green, near York, where she stayed for five years. Her poetry expresses her homesickness and unhappiness with her appointment. Brontë captured her experience as a governess in her novel *Agnes Grey* (1847), which depicts a young governess trying to manage spoiled children.

While at home between the two jobs, Brontë met her father's new curate, William Weightman. Her writings of this time suggest that she fell in love with him, but there is considerable scholarly debate over this point. If true, her feelings were hidden and almost certainly unrequited. Weightman and Aunt Branwell both died in 1842, and Brontë grieved through her poetry. In 1843, Brontë's brother Branwell joined her at Thorp Green to tutor the Robinson's son. Brontë resigned her post in June 1845—Branwell was dismissed soon thereafter for having an affair with Mrs. Robinson.

In 1845, with all four Brontë siblings at home and out of work, Charlotte, Emily, and Anne reached an agreement to secretly publish their poems. *Poems by Currer, Ellis, and Acton Bell* was published the following year. (The sisters used pseudonyms that preserved their initials but obscured their sex.) *Agnes Grey*, Brontë's first novel, was published in 1847 and her second, *The Tenant of Wildfell Hall*, was published in 1848. During this time, the family's health was deteriorating. Branwell drank himself to his grave by September 1848. Many contend that Branwell, in part, inspired the character of Mr. Huntington. Emily died of tuberculosis in December 1848.

Brontë was also ill and, seeing her own death coming, she asked Charlotte to take her to Scarborough, a favorite place of hers near the sea. Anne Brontë died there on May 28, 1849, at the age of twenty-nine. She is buried there, while all the other Brontës are buried in the family vault in St. Michael and All Angels' Church, Haworth.

# Plot Summary

## *Volume I*

### *TO J. HALFORD, ESQ.*

*The Tenant of Wildfell Hall* begins with a letter from Gilbert Markham to his brother-in-law and friend, Jack Halford. Halford and Gilbert had a quarrel when Halford revealed a secret, and Gilbert did not return the favor. Gilbert promises to make amends and tell Halford his biggest secret although it is a long story.

### *CHAPTERS I-V*

In the autumn of 1827, a widowed young woman named Mrs. Graham takes up residence at the derelict Wildfell Hall. Rose Markham and her mother visit, hoping to learn more about this stranger, but she is evasive. Rose's older brother Gilbert cannot stop himself from staring at her in church and a few days later his hunting takes him near her house where he saves her son from falling out of a tree. Their first meeting is awkward because she is so suspicious of him.

Mrs. Graham pays a return visit to the Markhams where she gets into several arguments. Mrs. Markham chides her for spoiling her son because she will not let anyone else watch him. Then she and Gilbert quarrel about the strengths and weaknesses of men and women. She declines an invitation to the family's Guy Fawkes Day party on November 5th. At the party, the guests gossip endlessly about Mrs. Graham. Gilbert flirts with his sweetheart, Eliza Millward, the vicar's daughter. After the party, Mrs. Markham chastises her son for showing Eliza affection because she does not think Eliza will be a good wife for him.

At the end of November, Rose and Gilbert visit Wildfell Hall and learn that Mrs. Graham earns her living by painting landscapes—and she signs a false name to the paintings to hide her location. A mysterious man comes to visit, but Mrs. Graham sends him away before her guests see who he is. Gilbert accidentally uncovers a painting of a dashing young man, which annoys Mrs. Graham. But she apologizes to Gilbert for her temper, and they part on good terms.

### CHAPTERS VI-XII

Throughout winter, Gilbert and Mrs. Graham —now Helen—run into each other and have many pleasant conversations. In March, Gilbert meets Frederick Lawrence, his neighbor, on the road to Wildfell Hall. Lawrence expresses surprise because he thought Gilbert did not like Helen. Gilbert has changed his mind, but he mistakenly believes Lawrence to be in love with Helen. Lawrence laughs. In mid-May, Gilbert, Rose, Fergus, Jane, Richard, Mary, Eliza, Helen, and Arthur make the day-trip out to the seaside. Gilbert enjoys talking with Helen while they walk and even follows her when she slips away to sketch. Gilbert realizes that

Eliza's chatter annoys him and that he may be falling in love with Helen.

---

# Media Adaptations

- *The Tenant of Wildfell Hall* was first adapted to television by the British Broadcasting Corporation (BBC) in 1968. It was directed by Peter Sasdy with a script by Christopher Fry and starred Janet Munro as Helen Huntington. The BBC aired this miniseries in four parts from December 28, 1968, through January 18, 1969. It is three hours long and available in limited quantities on VHS from the United Kingdom.

- The BBC produced another adaptation of *The Tenant of Wildfell Hall* in 1996. The script was adapted by Janet Barron, and the production stars Tara Fitzgerald as Helen Huntington. Mike Barker directed this highly rated adaptation. It is two and a half hours long and was originally aired in three parts. It is available on VHS from Twentieth-Century Fox (released 1997) and BBC Warner (released 2000). DVD availability is limited to Europe.

---

In June 1828, Gilbert tries to give Helen a new book, but she refuses to take it without paying because she does not want to encourage his affections. Gilbert is crushed but promises that he will not make any advances on her favor. She takes the book as a gift on those terms, and they part as friends. Not long after Gilbert's affection shifts from Eliza to Helen, scandalous gossip about Helen emerges and spreads rapidly among her neighbors. People whisper that she is involved with Lawrence and her child even looks like him. Gilbert refuses to believe the slander, but Mrs. Markham thinks there might be some kernel of truth. He visits Wildfell Hall the following week to lend Helen a book. They walk in the garden, and he asks her for a rose, which she gives him. Realizing his intentions, Helen implores him to be her friend or end their acquaintance. Gilbert reluctantly agrees and leaves, running into Lawrence on the road. They quarrel about why Lawrence is traveling to Wildfell Hall, but Reverend Millward interrupts them.

Back at home, Rose tells Gilbert to stop visiting Helen and soon thereafter Reverend Millward arrives. He has just returned from Wildfell Hall where he told Helen the gossip circulating and asked her to correct her conduct. He says she took the news badly, which causes Gilbert to immediately rush back to Wildfell Hall. He tells Helen he believes none of the rumors and that he loves her. Helen offers to explain her secrets to him the following day. Gilbert leaves reluctantly. Lingering outside, he chances to see Helen walking arm-in-arm with Lawrence. This view seems to confirm the rumor after all.

## *CHAPTERS XIII-XV*

Gilbert pours himself into his work and avoids meeting Helen. He rides toward the nearby town one day and meets Mr. Lawrence along the road. Lawrence tries to talk to him, but Gilbert is so angry that he strikes him with his horsewhip, cutting open his head and knocking him to the ground. After Gilbert makes sure Lawrence is still alive, he starts to leave, then he returns to offer help. Lawrence refuses, and Gilbert goes on to town, leaving Lawrence lying on the damp ground. When Gilbert returns home, Rose tells him that Lawrence has had a terrible accident. She urges him to visit Lawrence, who may be on his deathbed, but Gilbert refuses, sending Fergus instead. Helen finally catches Gilbert and asks him why he did not meet her to hear her story. They argue, and she leaves, but Gilbert grows curious. He visits her the next day and reveals why he is angry. Helen gives him her diary by way of explanation.

## *CHAPTERS XVI-XIX*

The next twenty-nine chapters are told from Helen's perspective, via her diary. Her story begins June 1, 1821, seven years earlier. Helen is eighteen years old and lives at Staningley manor with her uncle and aunt, Mr. and Mrs. Maxwell. She reflects upon her latest visit to town, meaning London. Mrs. Maxwell has introduced Helen to some older men, but Helen is only interested in the dashing Mr. Huntington. One of the older suitors, Mr. Boarham, proposes, but Helen refuses him. The next day, she visits her uncle's friend Mr. Wilmot and Huntington is among the guests. He pays special attention to Helen, which distresses her aunt. Mrs. Maxwell tries to dissuade Helen from forming an attachment to Huntington, but Helen believes she can reform him.

A party comes to Staningley in the autumn of 1821, including Huntington, Lord Lowborough, Boarham, Wilmot, Annabella Wilmot, and Milicent Hargrave. Helen is excited to see Huntington, but he confuses her by flirting with Annabella. She is brought to tears one evening when Annabella sings a song about lost love. Helen flees to the library to cry, and Huntington follows her, declaring his love and asking her to be his wife. Mrs. Maxwell comes upon them kissing, and Helen assures her aunt that she has not yet given her assent.

# *Volume II*

## CHAPTERS XX-XXIII

Helen is very happy the next day but she tells Mr. Huntington that her aunt and uncle will only let her marry a good man. He promises her to be better than he has been. Later, Helen talks with her aunt, declaring that she will reform Huntington when she is his wife. But at church that day, Helen observes Huntington's wandering attention and boredom. Nevertheless, she tells her uncle she will marry the man, and Christmas is settled upon for the wedding day, three months hence. Milicent is surprised at this engagement while Annabella declares her intention to become Lady Lowborough. Later that day, Huntington tells Helen a long story about how he and his friends mistreated Lord Lowborough while the lord struggled with a gambling problem and alcoholism. Helen is appalled at Huntington's lack of compassion. Before the end of the day, Annabelle and Lowborough are engaged as well.

Eight weeks into her marriage, February 1822, Helen is beginning to feel a little disenchanted with her husband. Huntington hurried through their honeymoon on the continent and, once home at Grassdale Manor, implored Helen to be less religious so that she could give him more of her heart.

## CHAPTERS XXIV-XXVII

In April, Helen and Huntington quarrel after he tells her about an affair he had with a married woman when he was younger. Helen thinks to herself, "for the first time in my life, and I hope the last, I wished I had not married him." Restless with country life, Huntington makes plans to go to London. He and Helen make up, and she accompanies him. She returns to Grassdale Manor a month later. Huntington stays behind to finish some unspecified business. He keeps delaying his return and reports in his letters that Milicent is engaged to his friend Mr. Hattersley. Milicent writes to Helen that Hattersley tricked her into the engagement, but Milicent was too timid to speak out against him. Huntington finally returns home at the end of July, ill from too much debauchery. He recovers after a few days and plans to have their friends come and visit in September: Lord and Lady Lowborough, Mr. and Mrs. Hattersley, Mr. Grimsby, and Walter Hargrave, their neighbor. Annabella and Huntington flirt together, distressing both Lowborough and Helen. A month into the visit, Helen sees Huntington and Annabella talking at the piano with hands intimately clasped. Helen is upset, but Huntington convinces her that it means nothing.

## CHAPTERS XXVIII-XXXII

By Christmas 1822, Helen and Huntington have a son, who is named Arthur after his father. Helen is delighted to be a mother, but Huntington is jealous of the time and affection Helen devotes to the baby. A year later, Helen is glad to see Huntington take an interest in little Arthur but fears that her son will take after his father. In the spring, Huntington says he is returning to London without Helen or the baby. He is gone from March through July during which time Helen visits with the

Hargraves for company even though she finds Mr. Hargrave annoying. Huntington is more ill this time when he returns home than he was the previous summer but a trip to Scotland to hunt refreshes him.

In March 1824, Huntington sneaks off to London while Helen is visiting her ill father. Huntington returns in July and soon thereafter Helen's father dies. Huntington will not let her go to the funeral because he wants her at home with him. In September, their friends visit again. Grimsby and Hattersley encourage Huntington to drink heavily, and the three men behave riotously and rudely to the rest of the company. A week into the visit, Milicent urges Helen to talk to her younger sister Esther about being very careful in her choice of a spouse. Hattersley complains to his wife that he wishes she would be firmer with him. His concerns show him to be more introspective than Huntington. Mr.Hargrave wishes to tell Helen some terrible news about her husband, but she refuses to hear him.

## CHAPTERS XXXIII-XXXVII

One night, Helen comes upon her husband outside. At first he is delighted, then surprised, and he demands that she return to the house. His affection puts Helen in a good mood for the evening. Two nights later, Helen discovers her husband and Annabella in the shrubbery outside, kissing and exchanging endearments. Later Helen asks him if he will permit her and their son to leave, but he refuses. Helen struggles the next day to behave normally. She makes her enmity known to Annabella, who begs Helen not to tell Lowborough. Helen declares that she will tell no one but not because Annabella asks it of her. A few weeks later, Hargrave declares his affection to Helen, who is offended. He apologizes later, but their conference is observed by Grimsby and Hattersley, whose looks imply they believe something is going on between them.

After their guests leave, Helen and Huntington grow accustomed to their estrangement even as they continue to live in the same house. Helen is distressed that two-year-old Arthur seems to cling to his father more than his mother. In May, Hargrave renews his declaration of love to Helen and is again rebuffed. Esther knows they have quarreled and is concerned that they remain friends. Helen is very annoyed by Hargrave. In November, he again tries to convince her to return his affection and, angered, Helen tells him he is selfish and should leave her alone. He soon leaves for Paris, and Helen is relieved.

## *Volume III*

### *CHAPTERS XXXVIII-XLIV*

A year later, September 1826, Helen and Huntington's friends return for a visit joined by Mrs. Hargrave and Esther Hargrave. Two weeks into the visit, Lowborough finally catches his wife at her infidelity, and they leave the next day. During the rest of the visit, Helen is appalled to see Huntington teaching their four-year-old son how to behave like his father—drinking and swearing. She determines to leave Grassdale. Hargrave again renews his love declaration to Helen. Grimsby spies him gripping her hands and soon Huntington bursts into the room and confronts them. Helen's name is cleared by Hargrave's reluctant confession.

In January 1827, Huntington takes Helen's diary from her and reads it, discovering her plan to escape. He immediately confiscates all of her money and valuables and burns many of her painting tools. Helen's plans are dashed because she cannot afford to support herself and her son on the tiny allowance Huntington gives her. In March, Huntington leaves for London, and Helen works to break her son of the bad habits his father has taught him. Helen's brother, Frederick Lawrence, visits and agrees to aid Helen in leaving Grassdale. Helen councils Esther to be careful about whom she chooses to marry and to not marry for love alone. Milicent and her husband visit Grassdale, and Hattersley tells Helen that he is weary of Huntington and that she is better off not having him at home. Helen encourages his resolution to give up drinking and be a better husband and father.

Huntington returns to Grassdale in September and tells Helen he is hiring a governess for their son. Helen dislikes Miss Myers and soon resolves to leave Grassdale, even though she is penniless. In early October 1827, she and Rachel secretly pack a few boxes and, with Benson's help, send them ahead to the coach-office. Rising early in the morning,

Helen, Rachel, and little Arthur flee Grassdale in a hired coach. Helen disguises herself as a widow and travels under an assumed name, Mrs. Graham. After a day-long journey, they arrive at Wildfell Hall, the childhood home of Helen and her brother, which Rachel also remembers. Lawrence reports to Helen that Huntington is looking for her. They get settled at Wildfell Hall although Helen finds her new neighbors to be nosy.

## CHAPTERS XLV-XLIX

The story returns to the present time, summer of 1828. Gilbert hurries to Wildfell Hall the morning he finishes Helen's dairy. He and Helen reconcile, but she tells him that they can never see each other again. He implores her to change her mind, and she finally consents that he may write to her in six months time, after she has moved to a new place. Gilbert leaves and visits the ill Mr. Lawrence, who is surprised to see Gilbert, but they reconcile their differences. Gilbert cannot talk to anyone about Helen's story for fear of word getting back to Huntington. Helen moves two months later, and Gilbert visits with Lawrence to hear about her. He also warns his bachelor friend against pursuing Jane Wilson for a wife because she is cold-hearted underneath her charming veneer and hates Helen. Lawrence is offended at Gilbert's impertinence but soon cuts off his visits to Ryecote Farm.

In November 1828, Eliza visits the Markham home to tell Rose, Gilbert, and Fergus that Helen is not a widow but has actually run away from her husband. Gilbert is shocked and hurries to Woodford Hall where Lawrence tells him that Helen has returned to Grassdale Manor to attend her ill husband, who has been abandoned by everyone else. Huntington has fallen from his horse and has internal injuries. Less than a week later, Lawrence shares another letter from Helen: Huntington is no longer delirious but is still unwell. Helen fears for Esther's happiness because her mother continues to push her to marry. With Helen's permission, Gilbert tells the truth to Rose, who spreads it to their neighbors. Two weeks later, Gilbert learns from another letter that Huntington's illness has returned. Hattersley and his family come to visit when they hear that Huntington is near death. Huntington is frightened and will not let Helen leave his side. He dies on December 5, 1828.

### *CHAPTERS L-LIII*

Lawrence leaves immediately to attend the funeral. Gilbert worries that the difference in social standing between him and Helen may yet keep them apart. He resolves to wait until the six months are up at the end of February to write to Helen. But near the end of January, Helen's uncle dies. Gilbert cannot write to her because he does not know the address for Staningley, and Lawrence will not tell him. In early December 1829, Eliza tells Gilbert that Helen is getting remarried to none other than Hargrave then laughs at him as he is overwhelmed with her news. Gilbert takes off the very next day for Grassdale, arriving at the church just as the newlyweds emerge. But it is Lawrence and his bride, Esther Hargrave who have been married that day and not Helen and Hargrave.

Gilbert travels to Staningley to see Helen. Near the manor he learns from his fellow travelers that Helen has inherited her uncle's estate and is now wealthy. Standing outside the manor gates, Gilbert decides they are too different in station, and he must leave her alone. A carriage drives by and Arthur spots Gilbert. Helen invites him into the house where he meets Mrs. Maxwell. When Gilbert and Helen are alone, they renew their declarations of affection for each other and make plans to get engaged and then marry. Helen and Gilbert marry eight months later, in August 1830.

# Characters

## Benson

Benson is a servant at Grassdale Manor. He helps Helen, Arthur, and Rachel flee from Mr. Huntington.

## Mr. Boarham

Mr. Boarham is Mrs. Maxwell's friend and one of Helen's suitors, but Helen refuses his marriage proposal because he repulses her.

## Master Arthur Graham

*See* Master Arthur Huntington

## Mrs. Helen Graham

*See* Mrs. Helen Huntington

## Mr. Grimsby

Mr. Grimsby is Mr. Huntington's friend. He lives for drinking, hunting, and gambling and is the only one of Huntington's friends who does not marry. He is eventually killed in a barroom brawl.

## Mr. Jack Halford Esq.

Jack Halford is Rose's husband and Gilbert's friend. *The Tenant of Wildfell Hall* is framed as a series of letters from Gilbert to Halford.

## *Miss Esther Hargrave*

Esther, the youngest Hargrave, is a friend to Helen. She is pretty and vivacious but suffers pressure from her mother and brother to marry quickly. She listens instead to Helen's advice: "When I tell you not to marry *without* love, I do not advise you to marry for love alone—there are many, many other things to be considered." At the end of the novel, she marries Helen's brother, Mr. Lawrence.

## *Miss Milicent Hargrave*

*See* Mrs. Milicent Hattersley

## *Mrs. Hargrave*

Mrs. Hargrave is mother to Walter, Milicent, and Esther. She is tightfisted and pushes her daughters to marry wealthy men while doting excessively on her son.

## *Mr. Walter Hargrave*

Walter Hargrave is the older brother of Milicent and Esther. He is spoiled but still more of a gentleman than his friends, Huntington, Hattersley, and Grimsby. Hargrave falls in love with Helen, but his love is egocentric and he annoys Helen. He eventually marries a plain but rich woman who is disappointed in him when his charm wears off, revealing his selfish and careless nature.

## *Miss Helen Hattersley*

Helen is the first child of Milicent and Ralph Hattersley. She is a few months younger than Helen's son Arthur.

## *Mrs. Milicent Hattersley*

Milicent Hattersley is Annabella's cousin and Helen's friend. Her gentle, yielding nature attracts the eye of the rakish Mr. Hattersley, who claims her as his fiancée almost against her wishes. Much like Helen, she is unhappy in her marriage for the first several years. Hattersley is often physically and verbally abusive. Milicent nevertheless believes that he is a good man and will eventually come around. When he does, they are very happy together. They have several children.

## *Master Ralph Hattersley*

Ralph is the second child of Milicent and Ralph Hattersley.

## *Mr. Ralph Hattersley Esq.*

Mr. Hattersley is Mr. Huntington's friend. For the first few years of his marriage, Hattersley continues to live a profligate lifestyle, but as he sees Huntington's health decline, he reforms his ways. Hattersley turns to his wife and family. He no longer goes to London to party, instead keeping busy at his country manor with farming, breeding cattle and horses, and hunting. He, his wife Milicent, and their sons and daughters live very happily thereafter.

## *Master Arthur Huntington*

The son of Helen and Arthur Huntington, Master Arthur Huntington is a cheerful little boy and innocently aids in bringing Gilbert and his mother together.

## *Mr. Arthur Huntington*

Arthur Huntington, Helen's husband, is handsome and charming but also irresponsible and selfish. Huntington regularly overindulges in drinking and gambling and has several affairs with other women, including Annabella Lowborough and Miss Myers. Huntington tires of Helen's pressure to reform and takes to spending several months a year in London or on the continent without his wife or son. Huntington takes no interest in Arthur except to be jealous of the attention Helen gives to the baby instead of to him. Even in the face of death, at the end of the novel, Huntington is childish and fearful, unable to seek solace in piety. Brontë, in the character of Huntington, has painted the portrait of a unmanly gentleman.

## Mrs. Helen Huntington

The heroine of Brontë's novel, Mrs. Helen Huntington courageously leaves her depraved husband to save her son from his father's influence. Helen is a religious and extremely moral person. As a young wife, she naively believes that she can cure Huntington of his profligate lifestyle and that he will welcome the change. When their marriage falls apart, Helen continues to stay at the house because Huntington has not given her permission to leave. She refuses the advances of Mr. Hargrave and Gilbert because she is still married. Hargrave's persistence offends her but refusing Gilbert is more difficult because she returns his loves; however, her piety makes it impossible for her to betray her marriage vows.

Helen loves literature—an interest she shares with Gilbert. She also loves to write in her diary and record events in great details, making the direct, first-person presentation of half of the novel possible. As a character, Helen has one glaring flaw: her infallibility. Brontë has made Helen too perfect. Even Gilbert, the other central character, is not entirely sympathetic because of his behavior. This excessive perfection gives one the sense that Helen is more acted upon in events than an agent in shaping them.

## Mrs. Esther Lawrence

*See* Miss Esther Hargrave

## *Mr. Frederick Lawrence*

Frederick Lawrence is Helen's brother and Gilbert's neighbor. He and Gilbert have an awkward relationship, even after Gilbert understands Lawrence's true relationship with Helen. Gilbert warns Lawrence not to marry Jane Wilson because he knows that Jane hates Helen and that her charm is all on the surface. Although Lawrence is offended, he takes Gilbert's advice. Lawrence does not approve of Gilbert's attachment to Helen and even goes to some effort to interfere with their acquaintance once Helen leaves Wildfell Hall. At the end of the novel, Lawrence marries Helen's pretty young neighbor, Esther Hargrave.

## *Lady Annabella Lowborough*

Annabella is Milicent's beautiful and vivacious cousin. She marries Lord Lowborough after Mr. Huntington and Helen are engaged. Annabella and Huntington later have an affair. Despite her charm, Annabella is cold and cruel to Helen, whom she views as competition. Lowborough is devastated when he learns of the affair, and he takes their children and lives apart from his wife. Annabella eventually elopes with another man and moves to the continent whereupon her husband divorces her. Annabella's new man leaves her also. She continues to live extravagantly but eventually dies in disgrace and poverty.

## Lord Lowborough

Lord Lowborough is a friend of Huntington's who gives up drinking and gambling because he cannot moderate his behavior. He is quiet and morose but sincerely wants a wife to love. He marries Annabella Wilmot but learns after a few years that she is unfaithful. They separate, and he takes their son and daughter with him. Lowborough eventually divorces Annabella when she elopes to the continent with another man. He marries a steady older woman who cares for him and his children, and they live the rest of their lives very happily.

## Mr. Fergus Markham

Fergus Markham is Gilbert's younger brother. He is probably a teenager during the narrative and often does and says insensitive things. Fergus grows out of this phase by the time he inherits the family farm from Gilbert and marries a vicar's daughter.

## Mr. Gilbert Markham

Gilbert Markham is the narrator of this novel, relating the story by letters to his friend and brother-in-law, Halford. Gilbert is a gentleman farmer, managing his family's business in lieu of his father, who is either absent or dead. Gilbert likes to read and have intelligent conversation, which inevitably draws him to his mysterious new neighbor, the widow Helen Graham. He falls in love with her, and although he senses that she does not want a romance, he is unable to keep himself from declaring his attachment to her. He mistakes Mr. Lawrence for a suitor and becomes insanely jealous, to the extent that he strikes the man a near-deadly blow. The attack is a turning point for Gilbert, who slowly begins to temper his emotions. Helen returns his feelings but refuses to act on them, instead sharing her secret with Gilbert: she is still married. While they are separated for eighteen months, Gilbert undergoes a subtle transformation. His love for Helen both mellows and deepens. He loses his desperation although not his motivation. He cultivates a difficult friendship with Mr. Lawrence. Gilbert also becomes painfully aware of the differences in their social stations as Helen is much wealthier than he is. When they are finally united, these differences pose no barrier. Many critics have commented on Gilbert's character as problematic: He is not an entirely likable and at the least seems undeserving of Helen's love. These incongruities can be explained in terms of Brontë's realistic style.

## Mrs. Markham

Mrs. Markham is the mother of Gilbert, Rose, and Fergus Markham. Mrs. Markham tends to go along with neighborhood views, including when the whole community is suspicious of Helen.

## Miss Rose Markham

Rose Markham is the middle Markham child. She is a typical young woman, gossiping with her neighbors. Rose marries Jack Halford, the man to whom the narrative of this novel is addressed.

## Mrs. Margaret Maxwell

Mrs. Maxwell, Helen's aunt and the only woman Helen has known as a mother, tries to impress upon Helen the importance of choosing a good husband.

## Mr. Maxwell

Mr. Maxwell, Helen's uncle, leaves his entire estate of Staningley to her when he dies, making Helen wealthy.

## Miss Eliza Millward

Eliza Millward, the vicar's younger daughter, is vivacious but shallow, conspiring with Jane Wilson to spread nasty rumors about Helen after Gilbert spurns Eliza. She later marries a rich tradesman.

## Miss Mary Millward

Mary Millward, the vicar's older daughter, is a quiet and reserved woman and the only one besides Gilbert who refuses to believe the rumors about Helen. Mary is secretly engaged to Richard Wilson.

## Reverend Michael Millward

Reverend Millward, the local vicar, is a well-meaning busybody. When he retires, he passes on his position to his curate and son-in-law, Richard Wilson.

## Miss Alice Myers

Miss Myers is a governess hired by Huntington to come between Helen and her son. Brontë also alludes to a sexual relationship between Miss Myers and Huntington. Miss Myers abandons Huntington when he becomes gravely ill.

## Rachel

Rachel is Helen's nurse and has taken care of her since she was a child. She chooses to accompany Helen on her flight from Grassdale Manor rather than stay behind and be tormented by Mr. Huntington.

## Miss Annabella Wilmot

*See* Mrs. Annabella Lowborough

## Mr. Wilmot

Mr. Wilmot, Mr. Maxwell's friend and Annabella's uncle, is one of the older men who pursue Helen. He seems oblivious to her indifference, which disgusts Helen.

## Miss Jane Wilson

Jane Wilson, the only daughter of Mrs. Wilson, is pretty and accomplished at piano, but she can also be small-minded and unpleasant. Jane pursues Mr. Lawrence, hoping to marry him and his money, but Gilbert ruins her chances by warning off Mr. Lawrence. Jane never finds another rich man to marry and lives out her life as a gossipy old maid.

---

## Topics for Further Study

- Brontë's novel was written and takes place during the early nineteenth century in England. Research the clothing fashions for both men and women of this time and place. What were the differences between the high and low classes? Prepare a ten-minute speech or a detailed visual aid that focuses on a particular area of fashion (such as shoes, jewelry, gowns, or work clothes). Do the clothes look strange to you? Do you see any connection with modern fashion?

- Huntington is an alcoholic who denies he has a problem. Findings from a 2005 survey in the United Kingdom show that 19 percent of men and 8 percent of women drink heavily at least once a week. Research alcoholism and learn what the danger signs of alcohol abuse are as well as the steps one can take to break the addiction. In small groups, design an ad campaign aimed toward raising awareness of teen drinking and directing people where they can get help locally. For your campaign, you can make posters, flyers, newspaper advertisements, and radio or television spots.

- In the early 2000s, domestic abuse remains a serious problem. Abuse does not need to be physical to do damage. Research domestic abuse in its various forms and read several case studies. How does Huntington fit the profile of an abuser? How do Helen and Arthur fit the profile of abused individuals? Write up the Huntington family as a case study in domestic abuse.

- Brontë's characters love to go on

walks. Sometimes they stroll in the garden after dinner and sometimes they take longer hikes (for example, out to the sea). Take a walk or hike of you own in a park or other scenic place, taking particular care to observe your surroundings. What do you see that is unique to that particular setting? What do you see that is familiar and unfamiliar? Do you see anything that pleases you? Immediately after your walk (or during a break in the middle of it) sit down and write a poem or story that captures your experience.

- Britain has its own cuisine, although it may not be as famous across the world as French or Italian cuisine. Research recipes for some traditional British foods. Do you see regional differences? How has British cuisine changed? Choose a dish to prepare and bring it to class to share in potluck fashion. Try a little bit of everything and discuss with your classmates what is unusual, what is familiar, what is unpleasant, and what you would like to eat again.

*Mrs. Wilson*

Mrs. Wilson is the mother of Robert, Jane, and Richard. Her older son Robert manages her home, Ryecote Farm. They are neighbors to the Markhams and the Millwards.

## Mr. Richard Wilson

Richard Wilson, Mrs. Wilson's younger son, is quiet and studious, and eventually he graduates from Cambridge. Richard is secretly engaged to Mary Millward, and they marry after he becomes curate to Reverend Millward. Richard succeeds Mr. Millward as vicar.

## Mr. Robert Wilson

Robert Wilson, Mrs. Wilson's older son, manages the family's estate, Ryecote Farm.

# Themes

## *Alcoholism*

Alcoholism is a chronic substance abuse disorder. People who suffer from alcoholism are so preoccupied with alcohol that they cannot function normally. In the United Kingdom, as of 2001, alcoholism afflicted 8 percent of the population. In Brontë's novel, Huntington and several of his friends are heavy drinkers. Lord Lowborough and Mr. Hattersley each reform their lives, unlike Mr. Huntington and Mr. Grimsby. Lord Lowborough and Mr. Huntington both particularly seem affected by traditional signs of alcoholism. They drink to excess often and are even driven to the point of drinking alcohol early in the day to help themselves feel better. Lord Lowborough sees that he has a problem and with supreme effort and willpower, overcomes his addiction. Mr. Huntington never really believes he has a problem and gradually sinks into poor health until he is overcome by an internal injury, resulting from a fall from his horse. His son, Arthur, is made ill by the very smell of alcohol, a physiological sign of his psychological abhorrence for the substance that has so altered his father.

Mr. Hattersley, although he drinks heavily with his friends, does not seem to be afflicted by alcoholism as much as by a lifestyle problem. Once he resolves to spend his time in the country with his wife and stay away from London, he becomes a happy man. Mr. Grimsby, by contrast, continues to live an intemperate life, gambling and drinking and eventually dies in a brawl. The message Brontë is sending to her readers is abundantly clear: overindulgence in alcohol leads to ruin whereas moderation or abstinence leads to happiness.

## *Piety*

Piety is the state of being devout, in matters of religion and in matters of social or familial obligations. The daughter of a minister, Brontë was a pious woman who nonetheless struggled with her devotion several times during her short life. In *The Tenant of Wildfell Hall*, pious characters are rewarded. Despite extraordinary hardship as a young woman, Helen is firmly devoted to her religion and its moral precepts. Against all odds, she ends up a rich woman, happily married to a loving husband. After she and Mr. Huntington are estranged but still living in the same house, Mr. Hargrave declares his love to her, but Helen is not the least bit tempted from her loneliness. She dislikes Mr. Hargrave, but she is also offended that he would suggest she violate her marriage vows because those vows were made before God and are sacred. Later, at Wildfell Hall, she also rebuffs Gilbert without hesitation for much the same reason except that this time her choice is much more poignant because she does, in fact, love Gilbert.

Other characters rewarded for piety in this

novel include Mary Millward and Richard Wilson, who marry after being secretly engaged. They are regarded by many of their neighbors and relations as dull and uninteresting, but Helen quickly forms a friendship with Mary, drawn to her sensibility and strong moral sense. Mary, like Gilbert, is one of the few people who refuse to believe anything scandalous about Helen without knowing her true background. They sense in her a good nature that is not easily bent to vice. Milicent Hattersley is also rewarded in the long run when her husband reforms his bachelor ways and dedicates himself to his family, his religion, and his home. Although wild as a young man, Mr. Hattersley, by his own declaration, was only waiting for someone to rein him in.

Brontë further emphasizes the importance of piety with her numerous biblical references within the story. It was more common in nineteenth-century Western literature to allude frequently to the Bible because of the central importance this text played in people's lives.

## *Marriage*

In nineteenth-century England, marriage was an extremely important institution. Many women were raised with the understanding that their job, as young women, was to secure a good husband. For some, good was defined variously, as rich or loving or handsome or titled. Women were encouraged to marry young and to have children. Although there was pressure on men to marry also, education and business experience were important for middle-class men, so that they could maintain themselves, attract a wife, and support a family. Husbands were often considerably older than their wives.

Once married, a woman was in charge of the servants and the children. Her husband was head of the household and responsible for managing the family's income. In a high-class home, as seen at Grassdale Manor, this responsibility would entail keeping track of rents and inheritance. In a middle-class household, like that of the Markhams, the head managed the family business—in this case, a farm. In Brontë's novel, marriage is first treated by many of the characters as a stepping stone to some greater goal. Mr. Huntington loves Helen's beauty and is perhaps driven by his own reckless nature (reckless because he could have married Annabella, with whom he later has an affair). Helen is misguided by ideas of romantic love and duty into the delusion that she can repair her husband's conduct. Hattersley declares that he wants a pliant wife who will not interfere with his fun, but the truth that comes out later is that he really wants quite the opposite. Milicent is too shy and deferential to argue against the man who claims her hand. Lowborough wishes to be married to ease his loneliness; Annabella wants to be rich and have a title. Jane Wilson also seeks wealth.

What the reader learns over the course of the novel is that marriage is not an institution to be taken lightly. Helen is the guiding light on this point because although she is firmly against Huntington once they are estranged, she does not leave him until she believes their son is in danger. Also, she returns home to nurse her husband when all others have abandoned him. Her example guides Esther Hargrave toward making a more careful choice in mate, although Esther's delay in marrying angers her family. Gilbert's love for Helen is somewhat tempered by consideration for her hardship and higher status, but these differences are ultimately not an obstacle because Helen returns his love. Although *The Tenant of Wildfell Hall* is not a novel written in a romantic style, it is still much about the courtship and marriage plot, about what realistically works and what does not.

# Compare & Contrast

- **1840s:** According to the census, the population of England numbers nearly 15 million people. Approximately 1.5 million—or 9 percent—live in London, the largest city in the world at this time.
  **Today:** As of 2001, the population of England is 49 million people. London is the most populous city in Europe and is inhabited by more than 7 million people or roughly 7 percent of the British population.

- **1840s:** Personal communication is accomplished face-to-face or by letter-writing. Mass communication is achieved with newspapers, leaflets, and broadsides.

**Today:** Cell phones and email are popular ways to communicate. Letter-writing via the postal system is increasingly considered archaic and slow. Mass media is centered on the Internet, television, magazines, and newspapers.

- **1840s:** The population of England is largely Anglican. Small numbers of Jews and Roman Catholics also live in Britain. Alternate religions such as Unitarianism and various other forms of Protestantism are on the rise.

  **Today:** According to the 2001 census in the United Kingdom, the British population is comprised of 71.6 percent Christians, 2.7 percent Muslim, 1 percent Hindu, 0.4 percent Sikh, 0.3 percent Jewish, 0.3 percent Buddhist, and 0.3 percent other religions. Approximately 15.5 percent of respondents declared no religion, and 7.3 percent declined to answer.

# Epistolary Novel

An epistolary novel presents itself as a letter or collection of letters. The form allows the author to write in the first person of the letter writer and to address a particular reader to whom the letter is addressed. This setup provides certain advantages and allows for greater intimacy in tone. This form gives the novel the semblance of fact; the text is a document and not made up or fiction. The use of letters in a novel is a way around the omniscient narrator, as well, because it permits the narrator to show other characters' points of view. The epistolary form was not unique to Brontë. Letter writing was the most important means of communication in nineteenth-century Britain, after face-to-face contact. This form was used by many authors of fiction from the thirteenth through the nineteenth centuries. The third-person limited omniscient narrator technique became more popular later in the nineteenth century.

*The Tenant of Wildfell Hall* is narrated in a series of letters between Gilbert Markham and his brother-in-law and friend, Jack Halford. The events of the story take place between 1821 and 1830 while the letters conclude in 1847, seventeen to twenty-six years later. Other documents appear in the novel: Helen's diary is the prime example. Her story as reported in the diary spans Chapters XVI through XLIV. The heart of the novel is told to Gilbert (who is telling it to Halford) through her private diary. Also, at the end of the novel, the author continues to present Helen's experience directly through her letters to her brother, Mr. Lawrence, who shares them and often gives them to Gilbert. This format allows the author to jump back and forth in time and to jump from one narrator to another.

## *Allusion*

An allusion is an indirect reference to something external to the text, which economically adds another layer of meaning to the text for the reader who recognizes the reference. Brontë's novel is rich with allusion, particularly allusions to the Bible and occasionally to other literature. Her use of biblical allusions enhances her theme of piety by drawing an explicit connection between scripture and its relevance to the story of these characters. For example, in Chapter XX, Helen's aunt tries to impress upon Helen the disparity in virtue between Helen and Mr. Huntington: "how will it be in the end, when you see yourselves parted for ever; you, perhaps, taken into eternal bliss, and he cast into the lake that burneth with unquenchable fire." The burning lake is an allusion to Revelations 20:10 and 21:8. Helen, along with Brontë's contemporary readers would understand this reference and the weight that it carries—Mr. Huntington is, in Mrs. Maxwell's view, beyond Paradise, even if he loves

Helen well.

An example of another allusion from *The Tenant of Wildfell Hall* occurs in Chapter XXX when Mr. Huntington is declaring to Helen that he will do what he pleases just as his friend Hattersley does: "he might come home at any hour of the night or morning, or not come home at all; be sullen sober, or glorious drunk; and play the fool or the madman to his own heart's desire without any fear or botheration." The phrase, "play the fool or the madman" is a reference to William Shakespeare's *Twelfth Night* (the fool) and *King Lear* (the madman). Readers who understand this allusion would then grasp the foreshadowing of Mr. Huntington's downfall, like that of the tragic King Lear. If readers know the texts to which an author alludes, then the text at hand gains in meaning by its connection to those other works.

## King George IV and the Regency Era

The Regency is the name for that period from 1811 to 1820 when the Prince of Wales served as prince regent in place of his father the ill King George III. King George IV reigned from 1820, when his father died, until his own death in 1830 at age sixty-seven. The prince regent was best known for his extravagant lifestyle—hallmark of the Regency era—which angered his father, King George III, who was known to be thrifty and plain. Prince George further upset his parents and Parliament by carrying on a romance with the Roman Catholic Maria Anne Fitzherbert, whom he married in 1785, even though several laws prohibited the union. The couple kept their marriage secret. In 1787, friends of the profligate prince sought and were given a parliamentary grant to pay off George's debts. The prince was forced by his father to marry Caroline of Brunswick in 1795, but after conceiving a child, George and Caroline permanently separated. Fitzherbert remained a part of George's life throughout this period, but their relationship was over by 1811.

George IV was interested in fashion and is known for popularizing seaside spas. He founded King's College London as well as the National

Portrait Gallery. He enjoyed food and drink, like Mr. Huntington, and this indulgence eventually took its toll on his health. Late in life, he suffered from mental illness, gout, and mild porphyria (an inherited blood disease). History has come to regard King George IV as a pathetic, bloated, irresponsible figure, not unlike Brontë's villain, Mr. Huntington.

Regency era styles, from fashion to architecture, are marked by elegance. Greek Revival architecture became very popular and women's fashion turned to fabrics that were lighter in weight and color with the French-inspired empire waist. This era was also marked by war—the Revolutionary War in North America and the Napoleonic Wars on the continent.

## *Queen Victoria and the Victorian Era*

Following the brief seven-year reign of George's brother, King William IV, Queen Victoria took the throne in 1837 when she was only eighteen years old. Three years later she married her first cousin, Prince Albert. There are rumors that Albert did not really want to marry Victoria but agreed to it because of her status and pressure from his family. Ultimately theirs was a very happy marriage. Over the course of her long life, there were seven attempts to assassinate or frighten Victoria, all involving guns, but these incidents were generally believed to be attempts at fame rather than due to conspiracy.

Albert died in 1861, devastating Victoria who wore black for the rest of her life. Victoria celebrated her golden jubilee in 1887 to commemorate the fiftieth anniversary of her accession. Ten years later, she celebrated her diamond jubilee, which included recognition that she was then the longest reigning monarch in British history. Victoria died of a cerebral hemorrhage in 1901, aged eighty-one. She was queen for sixty-three years.

The Victorian era was marked by technological and scientific advances such as the Industrial Revolution and Charles Darwin's theory of evolution. Railways were built across the United Kingdom, making cities more accessible to rural populations. Women gained the right to divorce and own property. The clean lines of Regency fashion for women bloomed into larger skirts, more frills, and bustles. The Victorian era is remembered for the strong sense of morality espoused by the queen —probably a reaction to the flagrancy of King George IV. The first world fair—the Great Exhibition of 1851—was held in London. Photography was displayed for the first time there and the glass and steel architecture of the Crystal Palace was a herald of modern architecture. The Great Exhibition was an enormous success, and these massive fairs became a popular attraction in the Western world for the next one hundred years.

# Critical Overview

Brontë's writing talent has long been overshadowed by that of her older sisters, Charlotte and Emily. Although their work was romantic, even gothic,Brontë favored realism in her novels, anticipating the shift in taste that occurred during the nineteenth century. *The Tenant of Wildfell Hall* was a bestseller in its time, famous for its controversial depictions of oppressive and unhappy marriages as well as the heroine's courageous effort to free herself. Brontë's sisters did not approve of her stories, especially Charlotte, who survived all of her siblings and was executor of Brontë's literary estate. This alone may be the reason *The Tenant of Wildfell Hall* went out of print and faded from the minds of the reading public.

*The Tenant of Wildfell Hall* was published in 1848, just one year before Brontë died. She published her works under the pseudonym Acton Bell, and many assumed she was a man. An anonymous critic for the *Spectator*, in 1848, describes Brontë's subject as "offensive" and her writing as rough: "*The Tenant of Wildfell Hall* ... suggests the idea of considerable abilities ill applied." The following month, a reviewer for the *Literary World* writes more favorably of Brontë's novel, although this person mistakenly attributes *Wuthering Heights* to Acton Bell. The critic describes the two novels as "crude though powerful productions" and goes on to criticize Brontë's depiction of Huntington, Markham, and other characters as unrealistic. Nonetheless, the review affirms Brontë's talent: "[i]t is the writer's genius which makes his incongruities appear natural." Interestingly, the reviewer also comments on the favorable reception these two novels have received, despite critical condemnation. The reviewer suspects the author to be a "gifted" woman.

Brontë responded to her critics in the second edition preface of *The Tenant of Wildfell Hall*:

> My object in writing the following pages, was not simply to amuse the Reader, neither was it to gratify my own taste, nor yet to ingratiate myself with the Press and the Public: I wished to tell the truth, for truth always conveys its own moral to those who are able to receive it.

She also deflects the question about her sex, stating, "I am satisfied that if a book is a good one, it is so whatever the sex of the author may be." This opinion was fairly radical in a time when works produced by women were more leniently judged than those produced by men. The likelihood of not being taken seriously was a reason for adopting a sexually ambiguous pen name.

Just over fifty years later, critics of the twentieth century also gave *The Tenant of Wildfell Hall* mixed reviews. A reviewer for the *New York Times* considers it "far from unattractive as a story, and full of moral energy and strong ethical purpose." But Walter Frewen Lord, writing for the *Nineteenth Century* in 1903 is disturbed by the casual manner with which the characters dismiss their own brutality toward each other. For instance, Gilbert Markham strikes Mr. Lawrence with a riding crop, nearly killing him, and Mr. Hattersley brutally beats Lord Lowborough. Lord also criticizes Helen Huntington as entirely too "blameless," which makes her too perfect as a heroine. May Sinclair also complains about Helen's perfection in her introduction to the 1914 Everyman's Library edition of the novel. Sinclair describes the novel as "unspeakably and lamentably dull" but still significant because it is "the first attempt in the mid-Victorian novel to handle the relations of a revolting wife to a most revolting husband with anything approaching to a bold sincerity." It is, in fact, Sinclair declares in conclusion, "the first presentment of that Feminist novel which we all know." Naomi Lewis gives the novel a lukewarm reception in her 1946 review for the *New Statesman & Nation*. She writes, "Virtue, not passion, is the powerful motive of the book," and "The characters have a kind of reality, but they are observed, not felt as the surroundings inevitably are." "But for all the force of its detail, the book is not great," Lewis concludes. In 1970, Louis Auchincloss compares *Wuthering Heights* to *The Tenant of Wildfell Hall*, noting their similar structures (a story within a story) and sometimes strained methods of imparting information (extensive eavesdropping and diary-keeping), and concludes that although they are not very different, the former succeeded and the latter failed. When the form works, it is praised, and, he concludes, when the form does not work, it "is given more than a fair share of the blame." In all, critics have continued to have their reservations about this novel.

# What Do I Read Next?

- *Agnes Grey* (1847) was Anne Brontë's first novel and was probably inspired by her experience working as a governess. In this novel, the title character struggles to control and teach the undisciplined children of her wealthy employers.

- *Jane Eyre* (1847), by Charlotte Brontë, is a famous English novel about a plain governess who captures the interest of her employer, Edward Rochester. But Rochester has a terrible secret.

- *Wuthering Heights* (1847), by Emily Brontë, is a famous romantic story about Catherine Earnshaw and the interloper Heathcliff. They passionately love each other but differences in their social station prevent them from being together.

- *Pride and Prejudice* (1813), by Jane Austen, is about the love and misunderstandings between Elizabeth Bennett and the wealthy Mr. Darcy. Austen was popular in her time and was a literary influence on the Brontës.

- *Oliver Twist* (1837-1839), by Charles Dickens, tells the poignant tale of an orphaned boy who stumbles upon misfortune after misfortune before finally coming into happiness. Dickens focused his writing on the underprivileged, in contrast to many writers of his day.

- *The Awakening* (1899), by Kate Chopin, is a slim novel about a smothered young wife and mother who casts off the constraints of her position as a southern socialite.

- *Best Poems of the Brontë Sisters* (1997), edited by Candace Ward, is a Dover Thrift collection of ten poems by Charlotte, twenty-three poems by Emily, and fourteen poems by Anne. Emily is arguably the best—and most prolific—poet of the three. Anne was also a skilled poet, whereas Charlotte's strength lay more in fiction writing.

- *A History of English Literature* (2000), by Michael Alexander, is a lively and comprehensive examination of a rich literary tradition. Alexander includes a discussion of the ever-changing idea of which works are classics, including what the term classic means.

# Sources

Auchincloss, Louis, "Speaking of Books: The Trick of Author as Character," in *New York Times Book Review*, February 1, 1970, pp. 2, 38.

Brontë, Anne, "Preface to the Second Edition," in *The Tenant of Wildfell Hall*, Oxford University Press, 1992, pp. 3, 5.

———, *The Tenant of Wildfell Hall*, Oxford University Press, 1992.

Lewis, Naomi, "Books in General," in *New Statesman & Nation*, Vol. 32, No. 808, August 17, 1946, p. 119.

Lord, Walter Frewen, "The Brontë Novels," in *Nineteenth Century*, Vol. 3, No. 313, March 1903, p. 489.

Review of *The Tenant of Wildfell Hall*, in *Literary World*, Vol. 3, No. 80, August 12, 1848, pp. 544, 546.

Review of *The Tenant of Wildfell Hall*, in *New York Times Book Review*, May 19, 1900, p. 324.

Review of *The Tenant of Wildfell Hall*, in *Spectator*, No. 1045, July 8, 1848, pp. 662, 663.

Sinclair, May, "An Introduction," in *The Tenant of Wildfell Hall*, by Anne Brontë, Everyman's Library Series No. 685, J. M. Dent & Sons, 1922, pp. v-viii.

# Further Reading

Alexander, Christine, and Margaret Smith, *The Oxford Companion to the Brontës*, Oxford University Press, 2004.

> This book is organized like an encyclopedia, with entries on topics, including names of characters, titles of works, places the Brontës visited, books they read, and more. Alexander and Smith have included the Brontë sisters' father, Patrick, and brother, Branwell, as well.

Barker, Juliet, *The Brontë's: A Life in Letters*, Overlook Press, 1998.

> Barker's book collects the correspondence of the Brontë family: father Patrick, son Branwell, and three daughters, Charlotte, Emily, and Anne—some of which was not previously published. These letters provide insight into the personalities of a very literary family.

David, Saul, *Prince of Pleasure: The Prince of Wales and the Making of the Regency*, Grove/Atlantic, 2000.

> David's biography is an engaging and detailed examination of the life and times of profligate King George

IV, who died in 1830. George was known in his day not only as a patron of the arts but also as a drunk and a lecher.

Hawkes, Jason, *Yorkshire from the Air*, Ebury Press, 2001.

This book of aerial photographs captures the beauty of the Yorkshire countryside in the north of England. The Brontë family lived in Yorkshire and were very attached to this landscape of wild moors, rolling hills, grand old manors, historic towns, and seaside villages.

Lightning Source UK Ltd.
Milton Keynes UK
UKHW02f1408260418
321688UK00014B/577/P